Why Do We Drive on Our Side of the Road?

By Stephen Rickard

Published in 2026 by
Norwood House Press
2544 Clinton Street
Buffalo, NY 14224

The painting on page 7 depicts The Storming of the Bastille, by an unknown painter. The painting on pages 8-9 is The Battle of Austerlitz, by François Gérard, dated 1810.

Printed in the United States of America

Library of Congress Cataloging-in-Publication Data:
Names: Rickard, Stephen, 1957-, author. | Atkins, Jill (Children's author).
Title: Why do we drive on our side of the road? / by Stephen Ricakard. Were all vikings bad / by Jill Atkins.
Description: Buffalo, NY : Norwood House Press, 2026. | Series: Phonics all-stars: phase 5c
Identifiers: ISBN 9781978578777 (pbk.) | ISBN 9781978578784 (library bound) | ISBN 9781978578791 (ebook)
Subjects: LCSH: Reading–Phonetic method–Juvenile literature. | English language–Phonetics–Juvenile literature. | Traffic safety–Juvenile literature. | Automobiles–Juvenile literature. | Vikings–Juvenile literature.
Classification: LCC LB1573.3 R534 2026 | DDC 372.465–dc23

CPSIA compliance information: Batch #CW26NHP: For further information contact Norwood House Press at 1-800-237-9932.

There are some things in the world that we just accept, without ever asking, "Why?"

In some parts of the world, cars must drive on the left-hand side of the road. In other places, they must drive on the right.

Have you ever wondered why this is so?

Did it happen by accident, or was it because somebody passed a law about it?

In fact, the true story is a bit of both.

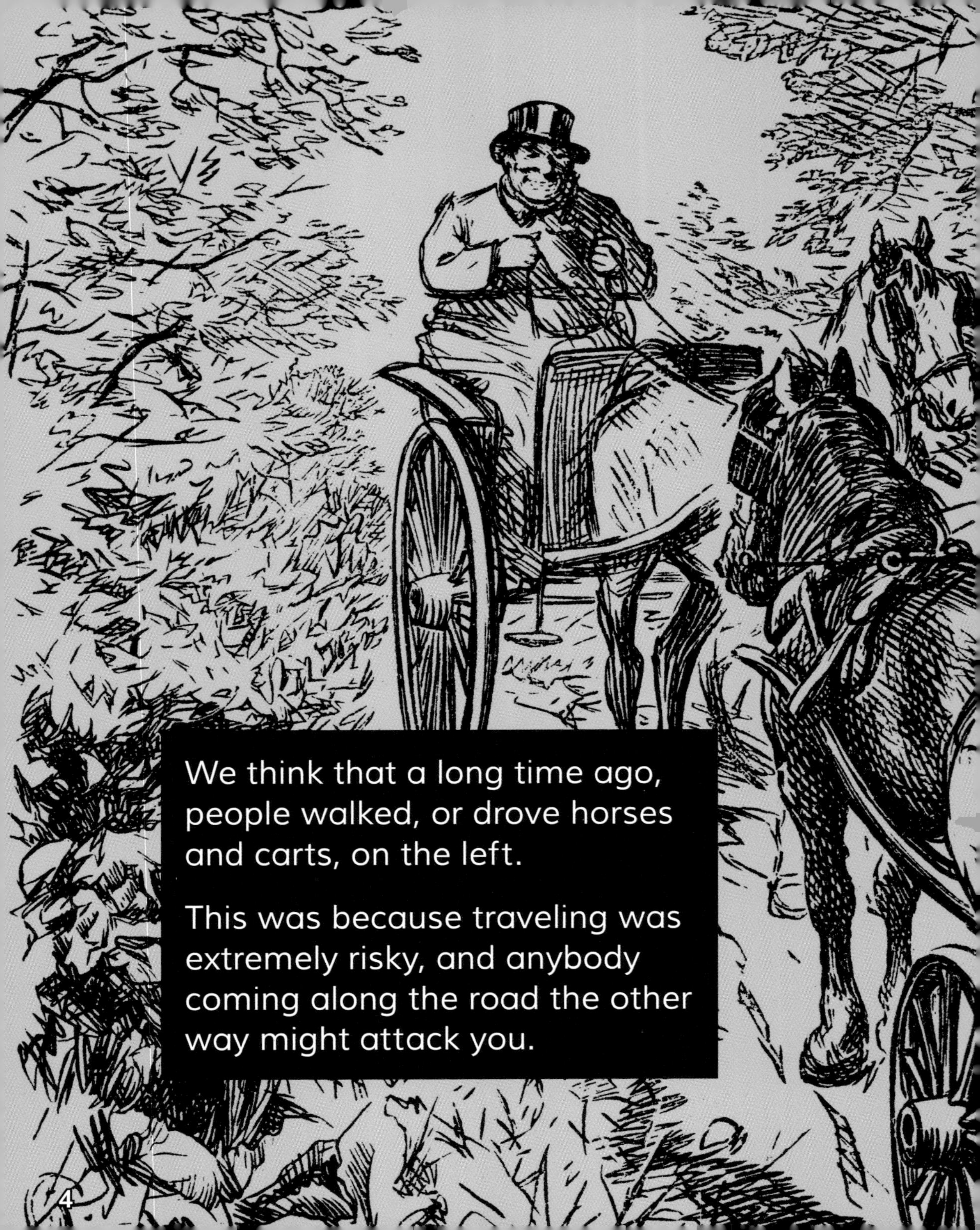

We think that a long time ago, people walked, or drove horses and carts, on the left.

This was because traveling was extremely risky, and anybody coming along the road the other way might attack you.

Riding on the left meant that your right hand (which might carry a weapon) was ready to defend you from any attack.

Since those days, many places have changed the rules, so now people in those places drive on the right.

Why?

In France, over 200 years ago, rich aristocrats rode on the left. This forced the hard-up people to walk on the right-hand side of the road.

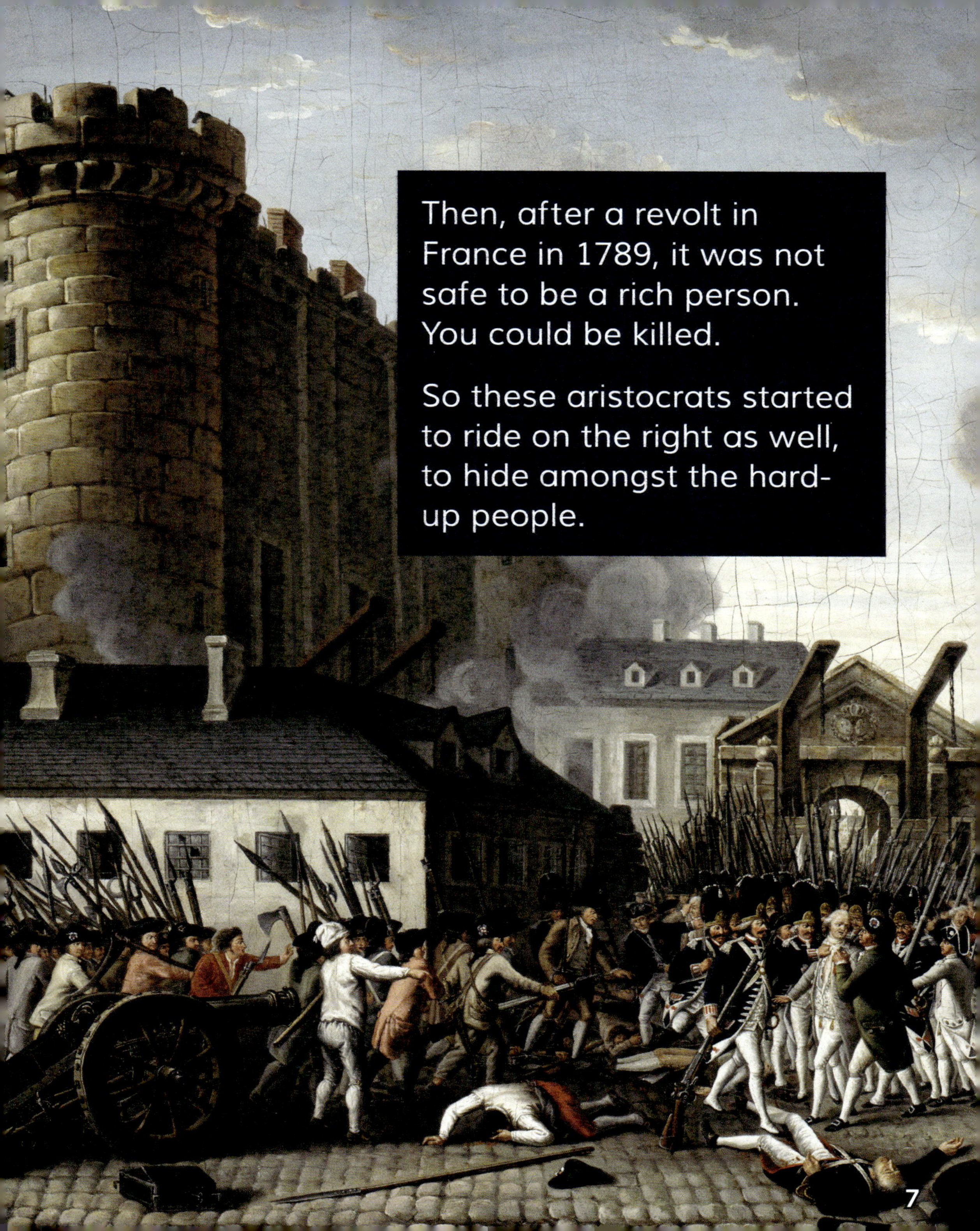

Then, after a revolt in France in 1789, it was not safe to be a rich person. You could be killed.

So these aristocrats started to ride on the right as well, to hide amongst the hard-up people.

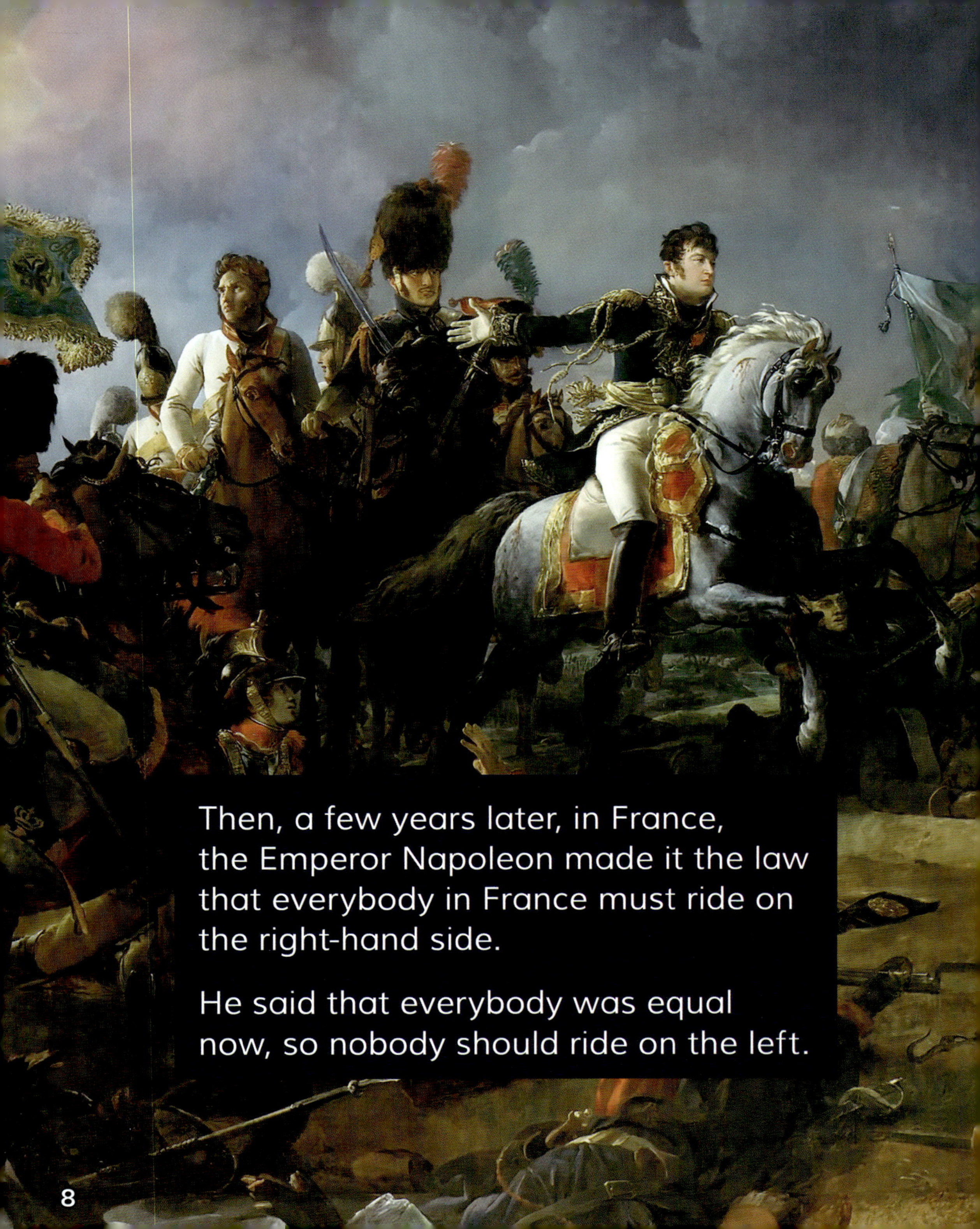

Then, a few years later, in France, the Emperor Napoleon made it the law that everybody in France must ride on the right-hand side.

He said that everybody was equal now, so nobody should ride on the left.

You must all ride on the right. We are all equal now.

When Napoleon invaded other states, such as Switzerland, Germany, and Poland, he made them travel on the right too.

The places that Napoleon did not invade, such as the United Kingdom and Portugal, carried on traveling on the left side of the road.

DRIVE
ON LEFT

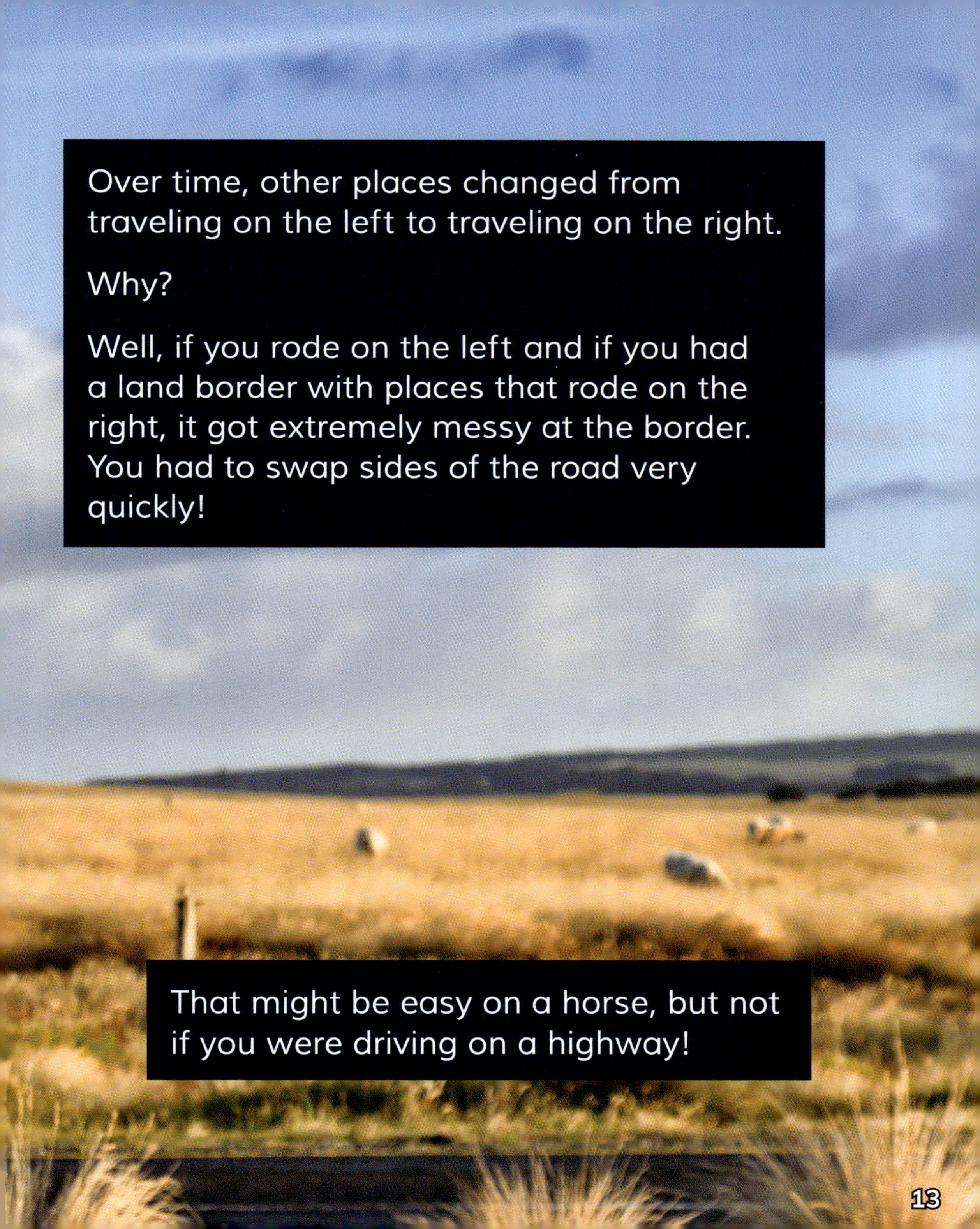

Over time, other places changed from traveling on the left to traveling on the right.

Why?

Well, if you rode on the left and if you had a land border with places that rode on the right, it got extremely messy at the border. You had to swap sides of the road very quickly!

That might be easy on a horse, but not if you were driving on a highway!

TAXI

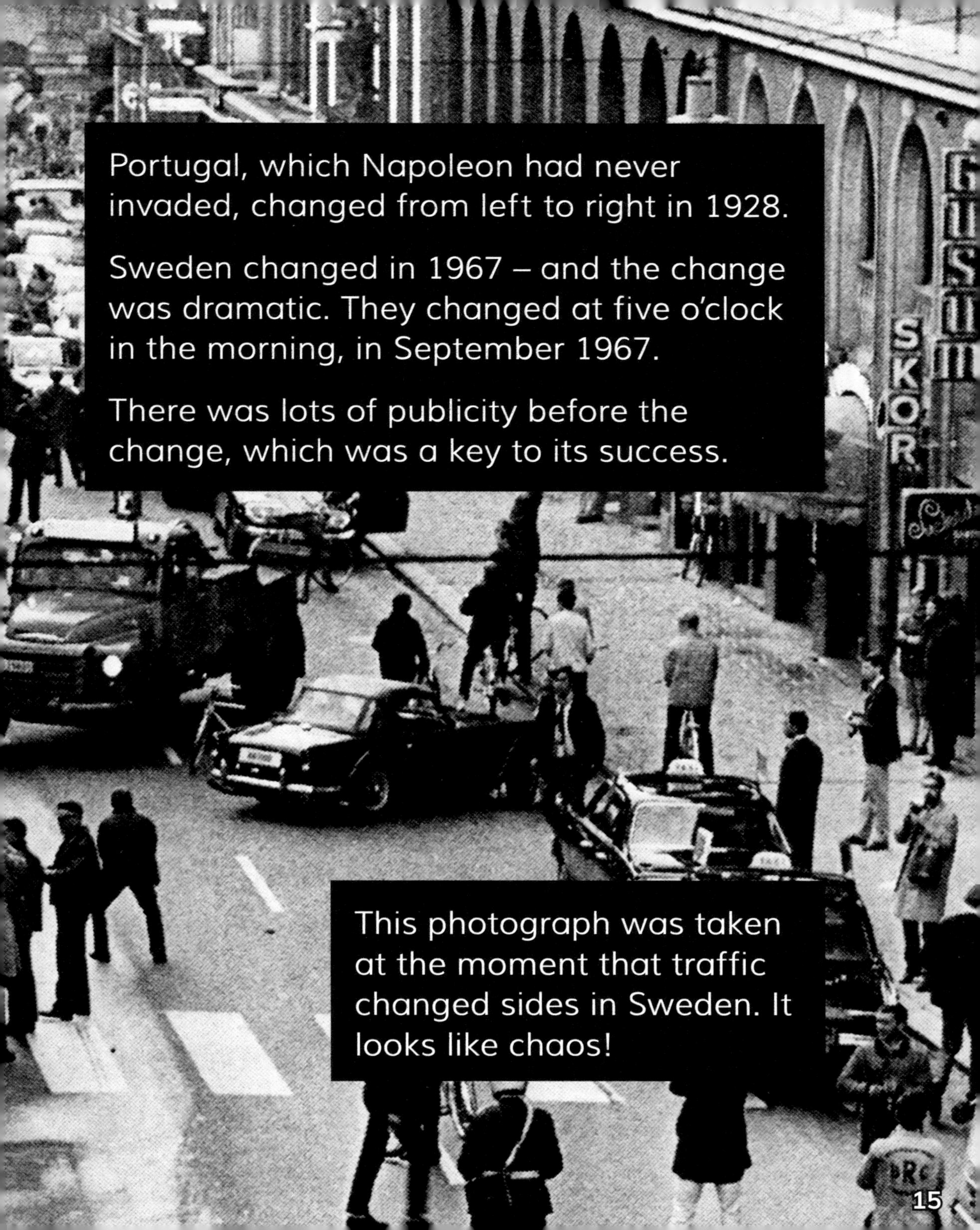

Portugal, which Napoleon had never invaded, changed from left to right in 1928.

Sweden changed in 1967 – and the change was dramatic. They changed at five o'clock in the morning, in September 1967.

There was lots of publicity before the change, which was a key to its success.

This photograph was taken at the moment that traffic changed sides in Sweden. It looks like chaos!

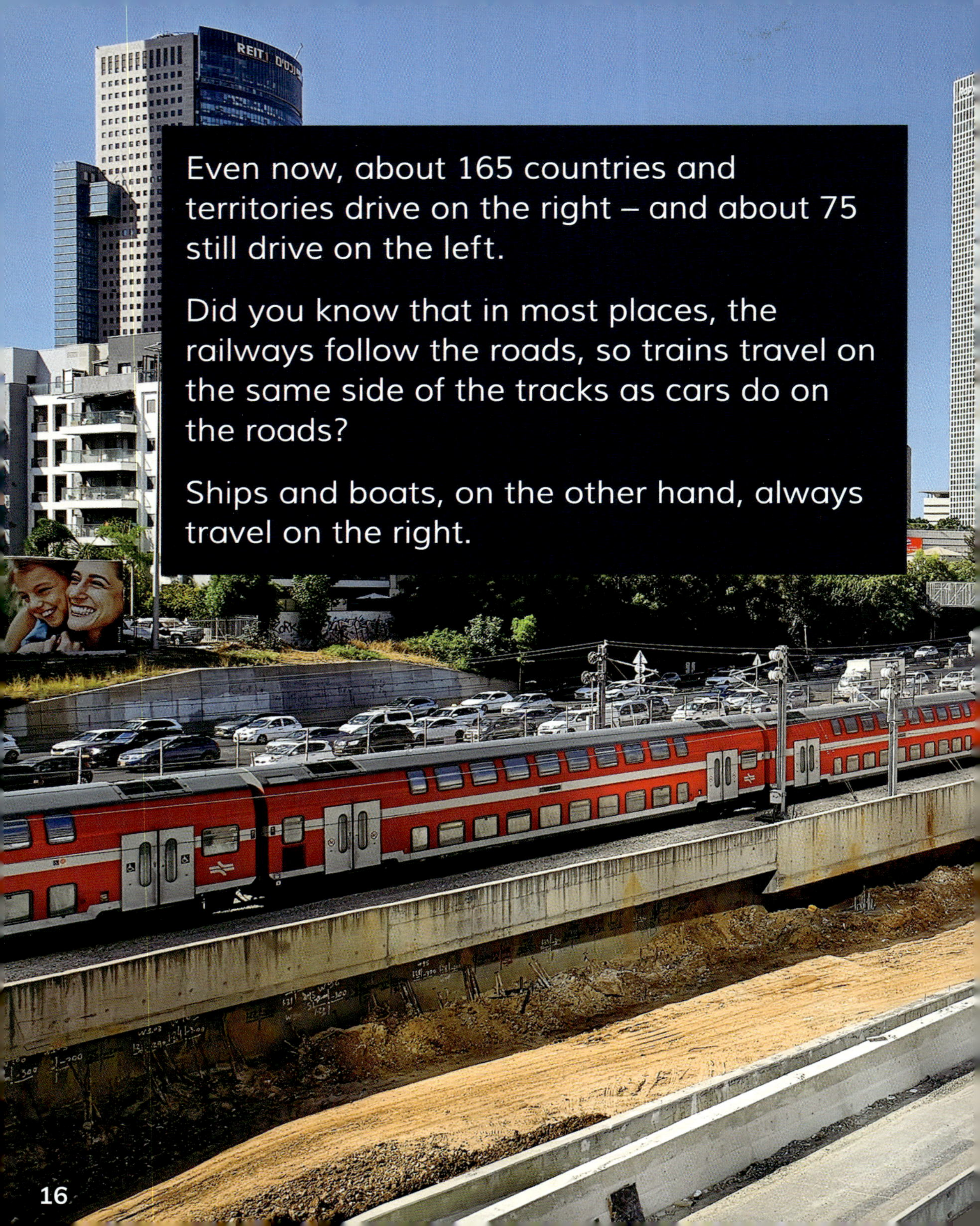

Even now, about 165 countries and territories drive on the right – and about 75 still drive on the left.

Did you know that in most places, the railways follow the roads, so trains travel on the same side of the tracks as cars do on the roads?

Ships and boats, on the other hand, always travel on the right.

Were the Vikings All Bad?

By Jill Atkins

We Vikings get really bad press.

We were Norsemen from Norway, Sweden, and Denmark, who lived over a thousand years ago.

It's true that we struck fear in people's minds.

Yet – if you think we looked anything like the rather silly picture on the cover of this book, then you are badly mistaken.

The word **Viking** means "pirate" or "raider."

So now people believe that all we ever did was attack and kill, taking all the loot and running off.

Well, some of that is true, I must confess.

One day, our chief was told about a very rich monastery sitting on a huge rock in the sea.

The rock was called Lindisfarne.

We put our axes, spears, and big round shields in the long ships, together with supplies for the trip.

Then, when our chief ordered us to raise the sail, we set off across the North Sea for Lindisfarne.

On Lindisfarne, we were fierce and ready for a fight.

Many monks were killed or captured – and we took the riches from the monastery. (I say that they started it when they came to our lands.)

That was just the beginning. We behaved quite badly after that.

We took on the Anglo-Saxons and, after much fierce fighting, we overpowered a good part of the mainland.

So, were we all bad? No!

We Vikings were explorers and traders as well as fighters. We traveled far and wide.

Why? Our homeland had many mountains and not much flat land.

We couldn't grow crops or keep animals to feed all our people, as crops and animals both need lots of flat land.

So, we had to find new ways to get food.

One way was to search for new places to live.

We traveled as far as a place called Greenland, which was mostly uninhabited because much of it was icy mountains.

One Viking explorer went even further, traveling across the Atlantic to what we now call Canada.

Yes, that's right. We were the first people to reach the "New World."

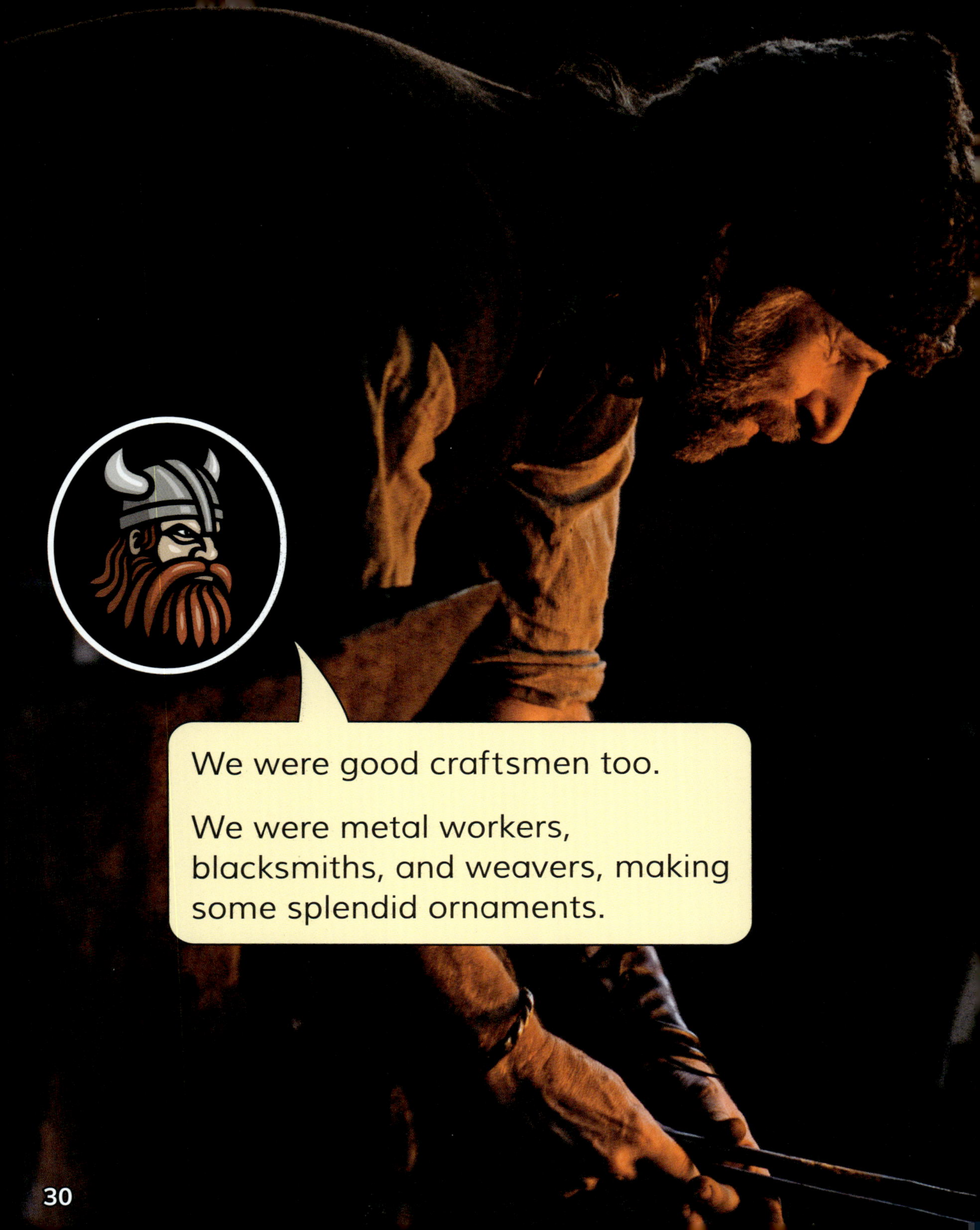

We were good craftsmen too.

We were metal workers, blacksmiths, and weavers, making some splendid ornaments.

We traded with peoples we met as well, bringing back silver, silk, spices, gems, glass, and pottery from many different places.

We made a lot of money.

How do you know that all this is true?

We left written records. (Our writing was a form of shapes and patterns called runes.)

Besides, people have discovered some of our weapons and coins – and even a long ship!

So – we weren't all bad, were we?